CLIL Readers

 Audio available

Where do you live?

written by
Amy White

Richmond

This is Emma.
She lives in the United States.

This is the city where Emma lives.
It is a very big city!

Where Emma lives, there are huge supermarkets.
They call them grocery stores.

Where Emma lives, there is a post office.
She likes to write letters.
This is where she posts her letters.

Where Emma lives, there is a big park.
It has swings, trees and grass.
The playground is what she likes the best.

Where Emma lives, there is a school.
She walks to school.
Some children take the bus.

Where Emma lives, there is a library.
You can take library books home to read.
Then, you must bring the books back. It is great!

8

Where Emma lives, there is a petrol station.
People can refuel their cars there.
Some people wash their cars there.

Where Emma lives, there is a bakery.
She loves the smell of fresh bread.
It smells so good!

Where Emma lives, there is a fire station. The big red fire engines have loud sirens!

Where Emma lives, there is an office building. A lot of people work there. Emma's mother works there.

Where Emma lives, there is an underground station. A lot of people use it.
Emma's father takes the underground to work.

Where Emma lives, there is a pizzeria. Emma and her family eat pizza once a month. That is a real treat!

Can you guess who lives here?
That is right!
This is Emma's house.

What is it like where you live?